W9-ANF-483

*E*ASY TO MAKE

NEW KNITTED TOYS

EASY TO MAKE

NEW KNITTED TOYS

JAN BIRD

ANAYA PUBLISHERS LTD LONDON

First published in Great Britain in 1994
by Anaya Publishers Ltd, Strode House,
44–50 Osnaburgh Street, London NW1 3ND

Editor Felicity Jackson
Design by Watermark Communications Group Ltd
Photographer Shona Wood
Illustrator Kate Simunek

British Library Cataloguing in Publication Data

Bird, Jan
Easy to Make New Knitted Toys – (Easy to Make Series)
I. Title II. Series
745.592

ISBN 1-85470-181-9

Typeset by Servis Filmsetting Ltd, Manchester, UK
Colour reproduction by Scantrans Pte Ltd, Singapore
Printed and bound in China
Produced by Mandarin Offset

CONTENTS

Introduction

Knitted toys are so easy that anyone can have hours of fun making them. This book holds a wonderful new collection from the very simple to the more difficult but all so easy to knit.

In the past it was generally men who knitted, either the herdsmen in the fields or fishermen. It was a highly skilled craft with a long apprenticeship, not the hobby it has become today. Unfortunately, due to the transient nature of knitted and untreated garments, the fabric wore out, so very little is known about the earliest forms of knitting.

It undoubtedly originated somewhere in the Middle East and was certainly around when the Vikings invaded Iceland in the 8th or 9th century. It was well established by the 14th century with knitted toys of a very simple form being made for the children.

Most people consider knitting a relaxing hobby you can do from the comfort of the armchair but in the Shetland Islands it is customary for knitters to carry their knitting with them whilst walking, and to do this they use a pad strapped to the hip in which they hold the yarn.

The yarns
These can be made from natural or synthetic fibres and sometimes a combination of both.

Natural yarns include lambswool and pure new wool, mohair, alpaca, linen, silk and cotton. Synthetic fibres include Acrylic, Courtelle and Bri Nylon.

Ply: This is a single strand of yarn which can be combined to produce 2, 3, 4, 5 Ply, Double Knitting, Chunky, Aran, etc. Sometimes in the spinning process a bouclé or slub, even lurex, is added to give a fancy texture. Softer yarns are spun loosely, hard wearing yarns such as guernseys are spun much tighter.

Tension

The majority of toys in this book are worked in Double Knitting yarn with a tension of 22 stitches and 30 rows to 4in (10cm) using 4mm (No 8) knitting needles. It is vitally important to check this before you begin to knit the toys (see page 74).

Finishing the toys

All the patterns in this book have instructions on how to sew the knitted pieces together. The various sewing techniques are explained and illustrated in the Better Techniques section starting on page 72.

Stuffing

This is a very important part of toy making; overstuffing can look as bad as understuffing. Fill a little at a time, moulding the shape of the toy as you go. Keep looking at the photograph to help you. When filling a very small or narrow piece of knitting, push the filling through the gap in the seam with the point of a knitting needle.

Be safe

Always use a good quality fire retardant filling when making toys for children. For small babies' toys, never sew on any decoration as they could easily pull them off. Remember, they can even swallow pompons. Always sew on ribbons or bows. Embroider features rather than use felt for toys for small children and never use buttons or pipe cleaners on toys that are intended for small babies.

STANDARD ABBREVIATIONS

beg	= beginning
dec	= decrease
inc	= increase
k	= knit
M1	= make one (see page 74)
p	= purl
skp	= slip one, knit one, pass slipped stitch over
st(s)	= stitches
st st	= stocking stitch
tbl	= through back of loop(s)
tog	= together
rev st st	= reversed stocking stitch

BRITISH AND AMERICAN KNITTING TERMS

UK	US
cast off	bind off
stocking stitch	stockinette stitch
tension	gauge
work straight	work even

ONE

Down on the Farm

Pond with water lilies

The pond is a traditional farmyard feature and this one is so easy to knit. If you wish, you could make it more fun by simply adding some felt fish, or even put a fence round it.

Materials
Patons Knit 'n' Save DK: 2 (25g) balls in blue; 3 (25g) balls in green; oddments of white and yellow for embroidery
Pair of 4mm (No 8) knitting needles
Medium size crochet hook
8in (20cm) square of green felt and small amounts of yellow and white for the flowers
Backing material to fit, approximately 21.5in × 13.5in (55cm × 34cm) – felt is best as the seams require no finishing

The water
Using blue, cast on 22 sts and k 1 row. Beg with a p row, work in st st as follows: Cast on 9 sts at beg of next row, 5 sts at beg of next row, 6 sts at beg of next row, 7 sts at beg of next row, 5 sts at beg of next 2 rows, 3 sts at beg of next row, 4 sts at beg of next row, 2 sts at beg of next row, 3 sts at beg of next row. Inc 1 st at beg of next row. Cast on 3 sts at beg of next row. Inc 1 st at beg of next row. Cast on 2 sts at beg of next 3 rows. P 1 row.
Next row: Cast on 2 sts at beg and inc 1 st at end.
P 1 row. Inc 1 st at beg of next 3 rows.
P 1 row. Inc 1 st each end of next row.
P 1 row. Inc 1 st at beg of next row.
P 1 row. Inc 1 st each end of next row.
P 1 row.
Inc 1 st at beg of next row. P 1 row.
Repeat the last 2 rows 3 times more.
Work 12 rows straight.
Dec 1 st each end of next row. P 1 row.
Dec 1 st each end of next row. Work 2 rows.
Dec 1 st at beg of next row. K 1 row.
Repeat the last 2 rows 3 times more.
Dec 1 st each end of next row. K 1 row.

Repeat the last 2 rows twice more. Cast off 3 sts at beg of next row, 2 sts at beg of next 6 rows, 3 sts at beg of next row, 2 sts at beg of next row, 4 sts at beg of next row, 3 sts at beg of next row, 4 sts at beg of next row, then 5 sts at beg of next 2 rows, 11 sts at beg of next row and cast off remaining sts.

The field
Using green, cast on 120 sts and k 3 rows.
Row 1: (Right side) K.
Row 2: K2, p to last 2 sts, k2.
Repeat these 2 rows for 95 rows. K 2 rows and cast off.

Finishing the water
Using the crochet hook and green yarn, work a row of double crochet all round edge of the water. Sew the field to the water approximately 3 rows from the cast on edge.

Lily pads
Cut out 8 lily pads from the green felt following the diagram and sew them to the water.

Flowers
Cut out 3 flowers from felt following the diagram. First roll a yellow piece, then secure the ends. Roll a white piece round the yellow centre and secure the ends. Sew on top of the lily pads. Embroider flowers around the edge of the water in lazy daisy stitch and French knots (see page 78).

Finishing
Sew the backing material in place on the wrong side of the knitting.

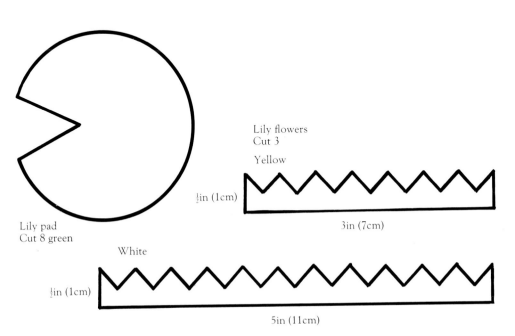

Lily flowers
Cut 3

Yellow

½in (1cm)

3in (7cm)

Lily pad
Cut 8 green

White

½in (1cm)

5in (11cm)

Cosy sheep

This lucky sheep will be so warm in winter with her lovely Aran coat. Or you could knit the coat in simple stocking stitch. Either way, she'll be cosy and cuddly and give hours of fun.

Materials
Patons Knit 'n' Save DK: 2 (25g) balls in
   white; 1 (25g) ball in pink
Pair of 4mm (No 8) knitting needles
Washable polyester toy filling
6in (15cm) square of pink felt; small
   amount of black felt for nostrils and
   eyes
Cable needle

Special abbreviation: C4B (Cable 4 Back
– see page 75).

Body (make 1)
Using white, cast on 5 sts.
Row 1: (Inc in every st) to end: 10 sts.
P 1 row.
Row 3: (Inc in every st) to end: 20 sts.
P 1 row.
Row 5: (Inc in every st) to end: 40 sts.
Beg with a p row, work 31 rows in st st.
Next row: (K2 tog) to end. P 1 row.
Next row: (K2 tog) to end. P 1 row.
Next row: (K2 tog) to end. Cut off yarn,
thread through remaining sts, pull up and
fasten off, join seam, leaving an opening,
fill and close the seam. Run a thread
round the cast on sts and pull up.

Legs (make 4)
Using pink, cast on 28 sts. K 1 row and p
1 row.
Row 1: (Skp, k10, k2 tog) twice. P 1 row.
Row 3: (Skp, k8, k2 tog) twice. P 1 row.
Cut off pink, join on white.
Row 5: (Skp, k6, k2 tog) twice.
Beg with a p row, work 11 rows in st st.
Cast off.
Sew the seam. Cut out sole shapes from
pink felt following the diagram and sew
to ends of the legs. Fill and sew to the
body.

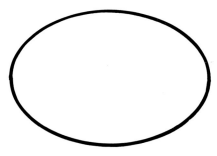

Sole (sheep, cow and donkey)
Cut 4

Head and nose (make 1)
Using white, cast on 28 sts and work 12
rows in st st. Join on pink and work 8
rows.
Next row: (K2 tog) to end. P 1 row.
Next row: (K2 tog) to end. P 1 row.
Next row: (K2 tog) 3 times, k1. Cut off
yarn, thread through remaining sts, pull
up and fasten off, join the seam and fill.
Cut out nostrils (2 small circles) and eye
shapes from black felt, following the
diagrams, and sew to the face. Sew head
to body.

Sheep's eye   Sheep's nostril
Cut 2 black   Cut 2 black

Ears (make 2)
Using white, cast on 6 sts and k 1 row.
Beg with a p row work in st st, inc 1 st

each end of next and following alternate row: 10 sts. Work 4 rows straight. Dec 1 st each end of next row. Cast off, decreasing 1 st each end. Cut out ear shape from pink felt following the diagram for Motif cow on page 20. Join seams, making a small pleat at base and sew to the head.

Work loops for hair in white yarn between the ears at the top of the head (see page 77).

Tail

Using white, cast on 36 sts and k 2 rows. Cast off. Fold in half and sew seams together, then sew to the body.

Coat (make 2)

Using white, cast on 38 sts and k 1 row. Work in pattern as follows:

Row 1: (P3, k4) 5 times, p3.
Row 2: (K3, p4) 5 times, k3.
Row 3: (P3, C4B) 5 times, p3.
Row 4: As row 2.

These 4 rows form the pattern. Repeat them for approximately 2½in (6cm), ending with row 1, for the other side end with row 2.

Cast off 7 sts at beg of next row. Work straight until work measures 4¼in (11cm), ending with row 2 or 4. Cast off.

Join seams, leaving an opening for head and tail. Place on the sheep.

Smart donkey

All ready for a ride on the donkey! His colourful blanket is made from felt but could just as easily be made from other fabrics or even knitted. Giddy up!

Materials
Patons Knit 'n' Save DK: 2 (25g) balls in
grey; small balls of black and pink
Pair of 4mm (No 8) knitting needles
Washable polyester toy filling
$3\frac{1}{4} \times 5\frac{1}{2}$in (8 × 14cm) piece of black felt;
small amount of pink, yellow and
white felt; $5\frac{1}{2} \times 2\frac{1}{2}$in (14 × 6cm) piece of
green felt; $6\frac{1}{4} \times 3\frac{1}{2}$in (16 × 8cm) piece of
red felt
18in (45cm) of ric rac braid for blanket

Body (make 2)
Using grey, cast on 40 sts and work $8\frac{3}{4}$in
(22cm) in st st, ending p row. Cast off.
Fold in half with cast on and cast off
edges together. Join lower seam and back
seam. Fill firmly and close seam.

Legs (make 4)
Using black, cast on 26 sts and work 2
rows in st st. Twist colours together to
avoid making a hole (see page 73).
Row 1: With black skp, k9, with grey k4,
with black k9, k2 tog.
Row 2: P10 black, 4 grey, 10 black.
Row 3: With black skp, k7, with grey k6,
with black k7, k2 tog.
Row 4: P8 black, 6 grey, 8 black.
Row 5: With black skp, k5, with grey k8,
with black k5, k2 tog.
Row 6: P6 black, 8 grey, 6 black.
Row 7: With black skp, k3, with grey
k10, with black k3, k2 tog.
Row 8: P4 black, 10 grey, 4 black.
Row 9: With black skp, k1, with grey
k12, with black k1, k2 tog.
Row 10: P2 black, 12 grey, 2 black. Cut
off black.
Row 11: Skp, k to last 2 sts, k2 tog.
Beg with a p row, work 11 rows in st st.
Cast off.

Cut out sole shapes from black felt
following the diagram for Cosy sheep on
page 12. Join leg seam then sew in sole.
Fill and sew to body.

Head (make 1)
Using grey, cast on 28 sts and work 6
rows in st st. Continue in st st, inc 1 st
each end of every row until there are 36
sts. Work 8 rows straight.
Row 1: K16, k2 tog, skp, k16.
Work 3 rows straight.
Row 5: K15, k2 tog, skp, k15.
Work 3 rows straight.
Row 9: K14, k2 tog, skp, k14.
Work 3 rows straight.
Row 13: K13, k2 tog, skp, k13.
P 1 row and cast off.
Fold in half lengthwise. Sew lower
shaped edge with cast on and cast off
edges together.

Nose (make 2)
Using pink, cast on 22 sts and work 4
rows in st st.
Dec 1 st each end of next and following
4th row, then on 3rd row: 16 sts. Now
dec on every following alternate row
until 10 sts remain. Cast off.
Join shaped edges and sew to front of
head. Fill head and sew to body.

Tail
Using grey, cast on 21 sts and work 4
rows in st st. Cast off. Fold in half
lengthwise and join seam, then sew to
body. Make a tassel in black yarn (see
page 77) and sew to end of tail.

Ears (make 2)
Using grey, cast on 11 sts and work 14
rows in st st.

Dec 1 st each end of next row, then following 4th row, then following 3rd row, then following alternate row: 3 sts. P3 tog and fasten off. Cut out the same shape in pink felt, join seams and make a pleat at base of ear, then sew to head.

Mane
Work a line of fringing in black yarn along the top of the head (see page 77).

Blanket
Position $5\frac{1}{2} \times 2\frac{1}{2}$in (14 × 6cm) piece of green felt on $6\frac{1}{4} \times 3\frac{1}{2}$in (16 × 8cm) piece of red felt. Cut out a $6 \times \frac{3}{4}$in (15 × 2cm) piece of yellow felt and sew together following picture, then fit round body. Sew braid to blanket.

Features
Cut out eye shapes from black and white felt following the diagram and sew to face. Embroider 2 small circles in black yarn for nostrils; work a line in black yarn for mouth (see page 79).

Donkey's eye

Cut 2 white oval shapes
Cut 2 black round shapes

Colourful cockerel

Have you ever seen such a colourful cockerel? And he is so easy to make from two circles of knitting! He's such a charmer you'll love making him and playing with him too.

Materials

Patons Knit 'n' Save DK: 1 (25g) ball in
    yellow; small ball of orange
Pair of 4mm (No 8) knitting needles
Washable polyester toy filling
8in (20cm) square of pink felt; 7in (18cm)
    square of green felt; 6in (15cm) square
    of orange felt;
2 buttons or felt for eyes

Body (make 2)

Using yellow, cast on 8 sts and k 1 row.
Beg with a p row, work in st st throughout. Cast on 3 sts at beg of next 2 rows
and 2 sts at beg of next 4 rows. P 1 row.
Inc 1 st each end of next and every
following alternate row to 26 sts, ending
with a p row.
Inc 1 st each end of next and following
4th row. Work 7 rows straight.
Dec 1 st each end of next and following

Place second piece of knitting on top and join seam

4th row. Work 1 row, then dec 1 st each
end of next and every following alternate
row until 22 sts remain. Work 1 row.
Cast off 2 sts at beg of next 4 rows and
3 sts at beg of next 2 rows. Cast off. Cut
out felt face following the diagram and
insert (see above). Join seam leaving an

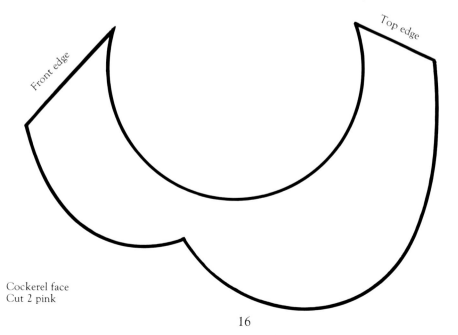

Cockerel face
Cut 2 pink

opening and sewing through all thicknesses, fill and close the seam.

Feet (make 2)
Using orange, cast on 8 sts and k 1 row.

(Cast off 4 sts, slip cast off st back onto left hand needle, then cast on 4 sts and k to end, k 1 row) twice.
Cast off. Sew the feet to the base of the cockerel's body.

Comb and tail

Cut out shapes from green and orange felt following the diagrams and picture. Join seams on right side and sew to each side of body, curving felt to fit shape of knitting.

Beak

Cut out shapes from felt. Join 2 seams with seam on right side (see diagram), fill lightly and sew to each side of the body.

Cockerel beak
Cut 2 pink

Cockerel comb
Cut 2 green

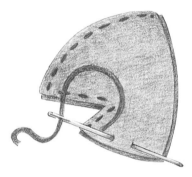

Sew felt pieces with seam on right side

Wings and eyes

Cut out wing shapes from green felt, following the diagram and picture, and sew to body. Sew on buttons for eyes or use felt.

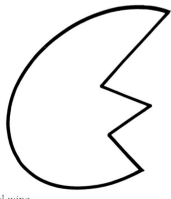

Cockerel wing
Cut 2

Cockerel tail   Cut 2 orange

18

Motif cow

Who could resist such an appealing face? If motif knitting is not for you, try making this lovely cow all in one colour, she'll be just as pretty.

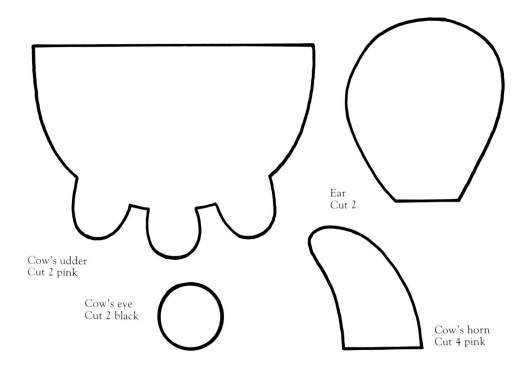

Cow's udder
Cut 2 pink

Cow's eye
Cut 2 black

Ear
Cut 2

Cow's horn
Cut 4 pink

Materials

Patons Knit 'n' Save DK: 2 (25g) balls in
    white; 1 (25g) ball in black; small
    amounts of pink
Pair of 4mm (No 8) knitting needles
Washable polyester toy filling
$3 \times 5\frac{1}{2}$in (8×14cm) of black felt;
    $6\frac{1}{4} \times 3\frac{1}{2}$in ($16 \times 8$cm) of pink felt
A small toy bell (optional)
10in (25cm) of narrow satin ribbon

Body (make 2)

Using white, cast on 20 sts and work
from chart opposite as follows:
Row 1: K.
Row 2: Cast on 3 sts, p to end.
Row 3: Cast on 3 sts, k to end.
Continue to work from chart (see notes
on motif knitting and working from
charts on page 74), casting on 2 sts at beg
of next 4 rows, inc 1 st each end of next
and following 2 alternate rows. When
row 22 has been worked, dec 1 st each
end of next and following 2 alternate
rows, cast off 2 sts at beg of next 4 rows
and 3 sts at beg of following 2 rows. Cast
off.

Join seams, leaving an opening, fill firmly
and close seam.

Head (make 2)

Using white, cast on 14 sts and work 2
rows in st st.
Cast on 3 sts at beg of next 2 rows and 2
sts at beg of following 2 rows: 24 sts.
Work 8 rows straight, then dec 1 st each
end of next and every following alternate
row until 16 sts remain.
Work 3 rows straight, then inc 1 st each
end of next and following 4th row.
Work 1 row, then dec 1 st each end of
next row.
Work 2 rows straight, then cast off 3 sts
at beg of next 4 rows. Cast off.
Join head seam, leaving an opening, fill
firmly and close seam. Sew head to body.

Nose (make 1)

Using pink, cast on 12 sts and k 1 row.
Beg with a p row work in st st, inc 1 st
each end of every row to 18 sts. Work 5
rows straight.
Dec 1 st each end of every row to 12 sts.
Work 1 row and cast off.

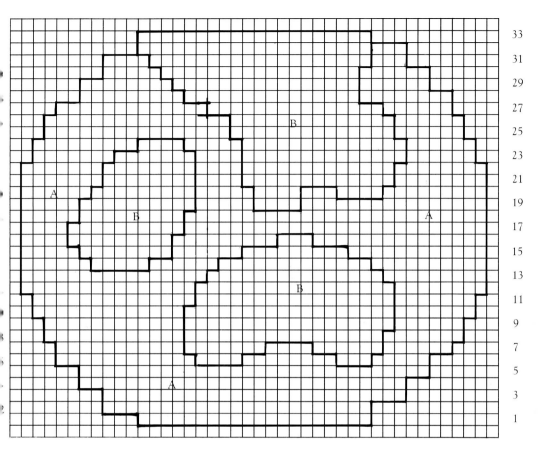

Cow's body

Key: A = White
     B = Black

Using black yarn, embroider a long stitch for mouth and 3 short stitches for the nostrils (see page 79). Fill lightly and sew to face.

Fringe
Work fringing loops on top of head as on Cosy sheep (see page 13).

Ears (make 2)
Work as for cosy sheep on page 12 in black and cutting out ear shape from black felt. Sew to head.

Tail
Work as for cosy sheep in white, make a tassel in black yarn (see page 77) and sew to body.

Legs (make 4)
Work as the legs of Smart donkey on page 14 but working white instead of grey. Cut out sole shapes from black felt following the diagram on page 12 and sew to ends of legs. Fill and sew the legs to the body.

Horns and udders
Cut out shapes from pink felt following the diagrams. Join the seams on the right side then fill lightly and sew to head and body.

Finishing
Cut out eye shapes from felt following the diagram and sew to face. Tie bell to satin ribbon and tie round neck of cow.

Cheery duck

Waddling along, this cheery duck is just ready for a dip in the farmyard duckpond. Why not make her a bonnet or an apron for her Sunday best?

Materials

Patons Knit 'n' Save DK: 2 (25g) balls in white

Pair of 4mm (No 8) knitting needles

Washable polyester toy filling

8in (20cm) square of white felt; 3in (7cm) square of yellow felt; 6in (15cm) square of orange felt

2 black buttons for eyes (if making for very small children use felt or embroidery)

20in (50cm) of ribbon

Body

Cast on 14 sts and k 1 row. Beg with a p row, work in st st: Cast on 3 sts at beg of next 3 rows, 2 sts at beg of next row, 3 sts at beg of next row, 2 sts at beg of next 2 rows. Inc 1 st at beg of next row. P 1 row. Inc 1 st at beg of next 3 rows. P 1 row. Inc 1 st at beg of next row. P 1 row and k 1 row. Inc 1 st at end of next row. K 1 row. Inc 1 st at end of next row. Work 3 rows. Dec 1 st at beg of next row. Cast off 17 sts at beg of next row. (Dec 1 st at beg of next row. Cast off 3 sts at beg of next row) twice. (Dec 1 st each end of next row. K 1 row) twice. Dec 1 st at end of next row. Work 2 rows. Inc 1 st at end of next row.

Next row: Inc 1 st at beg and dec 1 st at end. K 1 row. Inc 1 st at beg of next row. K 1 row. Cast on 4 sts at beg of next row. Work 3 rows straight. Dec 1 st at end of next row. Work 4 rows straight. Dec 1 st at beg of next row. P 1 row. Dec 1 st each end of next row. Dec 1 st at the beg of every row until 8 sts remain. Cast off. Work another piece in the same way but work in rev st st. Join seams, leaving an opening, fill the body firmly and then close opening.

Wings

Cast on 8 sts and k 1 row. Beg with a p row, work in st st as follows:
Cast on 5 sts at beg of next row, 2 sts at beg of next 3 rows. P 1 row. Cast on 4 sts at beg of next row. P 1 row. Cast off 11 sts at beg of next row. P 1 row.
Dec 1 st at beg of next row. Inc 1 st at end of next row. Inc 1 st at beg of next row. Dec 1 st at beg and inc 1 st at end of next row. Inc 1 st at beg of next row and at end of following row. K 1 row. Cast off 3 sts at beg of next 2 rows and 4 sts at beg of next row. Cast off.
Work another piece in same way but work in rev st st. Cut out the same shape from white felt. Join seams and sew to body.

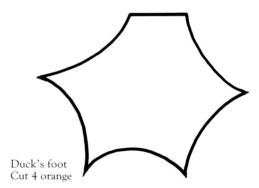

Duck's foot
Cut 4 orange

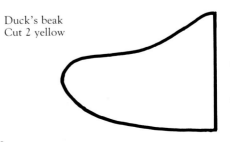

Duck's beak
Cut 2 yellow

Sew to face

Finishing

Cut out beak shapes from yellow felt following the diagram. Join seams on the right side, then fill lightly and sew to face. Place a marker on face for buttons and, using yarn, sew a couple of times through all thicknesses, pulling up firmly, then sew on buttons for the eyes. Cut out feet shapes from orange felt following the diagram. Join seams with right sides together, fill lightly and sew to body. Tie ribbon round the neck.

TWO

Cuddlies and Creepies

Baby teddy, Panda and Koala

This little bear has been knitted in the softest baby yarn with small hands in mind. Older children will find him just as lovable if he's knitted in the traditional brown bear shade. Panda and Koala are equally irresistible for animal lovers.

Materials

Baby teddy: Patons Fairy Tale DK:
  2 (50g) balls in pale blue; Patons Knit
  'n' Save DK: 1 (25g) ball in white;
  oddments of black for embroidery
Pair of 4mm (No 8) knitting needles
Washable polyester toy filling
Small amount of black felt for eyes and
  nose
20in (50cm) of 1in (2.5cm) wide satin
  ribbon

Panda: Patons Knit 'n' Save DK: 2 (25g)
  balls in white and 2 in black; a small
  ball of black mohair for inside the ears
Pair of 4mm (No 8) knitting needles
Washable polyester toy filling
Lock in safety eyes and a black 'panda'
  nose
20in (50cm) of 1in (2.5cm) wide satin
  ribbon

Koala: Patons Knit 'n' Save DK: 3 (25g)
  balls in camel; small amount of similar
  coloured mohair for inside ears
Pair of 4mm (No 8) knitting needles
Washable polyester toy filling
6in (15cm) square of black felt
20in (50cm) of 1in (2.5cm) wide satin
  ribbon
Lock in safety eyes

BABY TEDDY

Front body (make 1)
Using blue, * cast on 17 sts and k 1 row.
Continue in garter stitch as follows:
Row 1: Inc in first st, k7, M1, k1, M1,
k7, inc in last st.
K 3 rows.

Row 5: Inc in first st, k9, M1, k1, M1, k9, inc in last st.
K 3 rows.
Row 9: Inc in first st, k11, M1, k1, M1, k11, inc in last st.
K 3 rows. Inc 1 st each end of next and following 4th row: 33 sts.
K 25 rows. *
Cast on 7 sts at beg of next 2 rows.
Inc 1 st each end of next and following alternate row: 51 sts. K 1 row.

Row 1: K23, k2 tog tbl, k1, k2 tog, k23.
K 3 rows.
Row 5: K22, k2 tog tbl, k1, k2 tog, k22.
K 3 rows.
Row 9: K21, k2 tog tbl, k1, k2 tog, k21.
K 3 rows.
Row 13: K20, k2 tog tbl, k1, k2 tog, k20.
K 1 row.
Cast off 4 sts at beg of next 2 rows.
Next row: Cast off 3, k11, k2 tog tbl, k1, k2 tog, k to end.

27

Repeat this row once more.
Cast off 3 sts at beg of next 2 rows.
Dec 1 st each end of next 4 rows. Knit 2 rows and cast off.

Back body (make 1)

With blue ** cast on 17 sts and k 1 row.
Work in garter stitch throughout.
Inc 1 st each end of next row.
K 3 rows. Repeat the last 4 rows until there are 27 sts, ending with the inc row. K a further 25 rows. **
Cast on 7 sts at beg of next 2 rows.
Inc 1 st each end of next row.
K 1 row. Repeat the last 2 rows once more. K 13 rows.
Cast off 4 sts at beg of next 2 rows, then 3 sts at beg of next 4 rows. Dec 1 st at each end of next 4 rows. K 2 rows and cast off.

Ears (make 2 in blue and 2 in white)

Cast on 11 sts and k 3 rows. Inc 1 st each end of next row. K 6 rows. Dec 1 st each end of next and every following alternate row until 7 sts remain. Cast off.

Legs (make 2)

Using blue, cast on 32 sts and k 1 row.
Row 1: Inc in first st, k13, k2 tog, k2 tog tbl, k13, inc in last st.
K 3 rows.
Repeat the last 4 rows once more.
Next row: K14, k2 tog tbl, k2 tog, k14.
K 3 rows.
Next row: K13, k2 tog tbl, k2 tog, k13.
K 3 rows.
Next row: (K2 tog, k10, k2 tog tbl) twice.
K 18 rows. Cast off 4 sts at beg of next 4 rows and cast off.

Sole (make 2)

Using white, cast on 3 sts and k 1 row.
Inc 1 st each end of next and every following alternate row until there are 9 sts. K 7 rows. Dec 1 st each end of next and every following alternate row until 3 sts remain. Cast off.

Head (make 2)

Using blue, cast on 14 sts and k 1 row.
Inc 1 st each end of next 2 rows, then every following alternate row until there are 22 sts, then on following 4th row: 24 sts. K 17 rows. Dec 1 st each end of next and following 4th row, then following alternate row, then every row until 14 sts remain. Cast off.

Face (make 1)

Using white, cast on 15 sts.
Work in st st. K 1 row.
Inc 1 st each end of next 2 rows, then following alternate row: 21 sts. Work 3 rows straight. Dec 1 st each end of next and following alternate row, then following 2 rows. Cast off.

Finishing

Sew body pieces together leaving an opening. Fill and close opening. Sew a line through all thicknesses across top of arms. Join leg seams, sew in soles, fill and sew to body. Join head seam, leaving cast on edge open. Fill and sew to body. Sew on face, filling very lightly. Cut out eye and nose shapes from felt following the diagrams and sew to head. Using black yarn, embroider mouth (see page 78). Join ear seams, making a small pleat at base (see picture on previous page) and sew to head. Tie ribbon round neck.

Teddy's nose
Cut 1 black

Teddy's eye
Cut 2 black
(or use lock in eyes)

PANDA

Front body (make 1)

Using white, work as front body of Baby teddy on page 26 from * to *. Cut off white, join on black and complete as for teddy.

Back body

Using white, work as back of teddy from ** to **. Cut off white, join on black and complete as for teddy.

28

Legs
Work as for legs of teddy using black.

Soles
Work as for soles of teddy using black.

Ears
Work as for ears of teddy, making 2 in black DK and 2 in black mohair.

Head (make 2)
Using white, cast on 14 sts and k 1 row.
Work in garter stitch throughout.
Row 1: K, inc 1 st each end.
Row 2 and every following alternate row: K.
Row 3: Inc in first st, k to end.
Row 5: As row 1.
Row 7: As row 3.
Row 9: As row 1.
Row 11: K.
Row 13: As row 1.
Row 15: K.
Row 17: As row 1.
K 3 rows.
Shape nose:
Next row: Cast off 7, k to last 2 sts, k2 tog.
K 1 row.
Next row: K, dec 1 st each end.
K 1 row.
Repeat the last 2 rows until 8 sts remain.
Cast off.

Head gusset (make 1)
Using white, cast on 10 sts and k 5 rows.
Work in garter stitch throughout.
Next row: K, inc 1 st each end.
K 5 rows.
Repeat the last 6 rows twice more.
K 17 rows.
Next row: K, dec 1 st each end.
K 7 rows.
Repeat the last 8 rows three times more.
Dec 1 st each end of next row. K 11 rows. Dec 1 st each end of next row and cast off.

Eye patches (make 2)
Using black, cast on 6 sts and k 1 row.
Work in garter stitch as follows:
Row 1: K2 tog, k to last st, inc.

Row 2 and every following alternate row: K.
Row 3: K to last st, inc.
Row 5: As row 1.
Row 7: As row 3.
Row 9: As row 1.
Rows 11, 13 and 15: K, dec 1 st each end.
Cast off.

Finishing
Body and legs: Work as given for teddy.
Sew head gusset to head pieces beginning at centre back neck. Fill and sew to body.
Sew on eye patches and fix in eyes, sewing a thread through all thicknesses and pull up to indent eyes. Fix on nose.
Join ears, making a small pleat and sew to head. Embroider mouth (see page 78) and tie on ribbon.

KOALA

To make
Work all pieces as Panda, but use one colour throughout and work ears as follows: work 2 pieces in camel and 2 pieces in mohair.

Finishing
Work as for the panda but cut out nose and claw shapes from felt following diagrams. Sew 2 claw pieces together and insert claws to feet and paws before sewing seams. (See the diagram for Colourful cockerel on page 16). Sew on the nose piece.

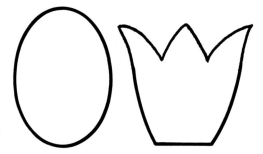

Koala's nose
Cut 1 black

Koala's claws
Cut 8 black

Scary dinosaur

Terrifyingly realistic, this Jurassic specimen of a tyrannic reptile is guaranteed to scare you and your friends witless, but don't be too worried, he is house-trained!

Materials

Patons Knit 'n' Save DK: 2 (25g) balls in pink and 2 in lime green
Pair of 4mm (No 8) knitting needles
Washable polyester toy filling
17½in (45cm) length of white felt; 6in (15cm) square each of yellow and pink felt; small amount of black felt

Body

Using pink, cast on 33 sts and knit 1 row.
Beg with a p row and work in st st throughout: Cast on 2 sts at beg of next row and 4 sts at beg of next row.
(Cast on 1 st at beg of next row and 2 sts at beg of following row) 4 times.
P 1 row. Inc 1 st each end of next row.
P 1 row. Inc 1 st at beg of next and following alternate row.
Next row: P38, cast off 7, p to end.
K 1 row. Cast off 5 sts at beg of next row.
K 1 row. Cast off 2 sts at beg of next row.
K 1 row. Cast off.
With right side facing, join on yarn and cast off 2 sts, then k remaining sts.
P 1 row. Cast off 2 sts at beg of next row.
P 1 row. Dec 1 st at beg of next row.
Work 4 rows straight.
Dec 1 st at end of next row.
Work 12 rows straight.
Dec 1 st at end of next and following 4th row, then every following alternate row until 28 sts remain. P 1 row.
Dec 1 st each end of next row.
Cast off 2 sts at beg of next row.
Dec 1 st at beg of next row.
Cast off 4 sts at beg of next row. Mark beg of this row with a coloured thread.
Inc 1 st at beg of next row.
Cast on 2 sts at beg of next row.
Inc 1 st at beg of next and every following alternate row until there are 26 sts. Work 3 rows straight.
Inc 1 st at beg of next row.
Work 5 rows straight.
Dec 1 st at beg of next row. Mark end of this row with a coloured thread.
Cast off 2 sts at beg of next row.
Dec 1 st at beg of next row.
Cast off 3 sts at beg of next row.
Cast off 2 sts at beg of next row, then 4 sts at beg of next row. Repeat the last 2 rows once more. Cast off.
Work another piece in same way, but reverse shapings by working in rev st st.
Cut out spine from white felt following diagram on page 34 and sew to one side of knitting down the back with straight edge to edge of knitting. Join front, head (leaving row ends between markers open), back and tail seams as far as cast on edge. Fill the body.

Tummy (make 1)

Using lime green, cast on 6 sts and k 1 row. Beg with a p row work in st st throughout. Cast on 3 sts at beg of next 2 rows, cast on 2 sts at beg of next 2 rows.
Inc 1 st each end of next and every following alternate row until there are 22 sts. Work 3 rows straight.
Inc 1 st each end of next row.
Work 6 rows straight.
Dec 1 st each end of next row.
Work 3 rows straight.
Dec 1 st each end of next and following 2 alternate rows.
Cast off 2 sts at beg of next 4 rows.
Work 1 row and cast off.
Fill lightly and sew to front of body.

Base (make 1)

* Using pink, cast on 7 sts and k 1 row.
Beg with a p row work in st st

throughout. Cast on 2 sts at beg of next 8 rows.
Inc 1 st each end of next row. *
Work 10 rows straight.
** Dec 1 st each end of next row.
Cast off 2 sts at beg of next 2 rows. Cast off.
Join shaped edges together. **
Sew base to body then close openings.

Nose (make 2)
Using lime green, work as base from * to *. Work 2 rows straight. Work as base from ** to **. Join shaped seams, fill and sew to straight edge of face between markers. Embroider 2 nostrils and a mouth in black yarn (see page 78). Cut out 2 horns from pink felt following the diagram for Motif cow on page 20, sew seams together, fill and sew to top of nose.

Cheeks (make 2)
Using lime green, cast on 10 sts and k 1 row. Beg with a p row, work in st st throughout. Cast on 3 sts at beg of next and following alternate row.
Work 1 row.

33

Inc 1 st at beg of next row.
Work 5 rows straight.
Dec 1 st at beg of next row. Work 1 row.
Cast off 2 sts at beg of next row and 3 sts
at beg of following 2 alternate rows. Cast
off. Work another piece in same way but
reverse shapings by working in rev st st.
Fill and sew to face.

Legs (make 2)

Using lime green, cast on 44 sts and work
8 rows in st st.
Dec 1 st each end of next row.
Cast off 2 sts at beg of next 2 rows.
Cast off 4 sts at beg of next 2 rows.
Cast off 6 sts at beg of next 2 rows.
Work 5 rows straight.
Cast off 4 sts at beg of next 2 rows. Cast
off.

Sole (make 2)

Using lime green, cast on 6 sts and k 1
row. Beg with a p row, work in st st, inc
1 st each end of next and following 2
alternate rows.
Work 11 rows straight.
Dec 1 st each end of next and following 2
alternate rows. Work 1 row and cast off.
Join front leg seam. Cut out claw shapes
from felt (4 triangles in white) and sew to
base of leg. Sew in the sole. Fill and sew
to body.

Dinosaur's spots

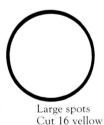

Small spots
Cut 16 yellow and 8 pink

Large spots
Cut 16 yellow

Foreleg (make 2)

Using lime green, cast on 5 sts and k 1
row. Beg with a p row, work in st st
throughout. Cast on 2 sts at beg of next 2
rows.
Inc 1 st at beg of next row.
Cast on 2 sts at beg of next row.
Inc 1 st at beg of next 2 rows.
P 1 row.
Inc 1 st at beg of next row.
Work 2 rows.
Cast off 3 sts at beg of next row and 2 sts
at beg of following alternate row.
Work 6 rows straight.
Cast off 4 sts at beg of next row.
P 1 row. Cast off.
Work another piece in same way but
reverse shapings by working in rev st st.
Cut out claws from felt (3 triangles in
white) and sew to leg. Join the seam, fill
lightly and sew to body.

Finishing

Cut out eye shapes from felt following
the diagram and glue or sew to face. Cut
out spots from felt following the diagram
and glue or sew on to body and tummy.

Dinosaur's eye

Cut 2 yellow

Cut 2 white

Cut 2 black

Finished eye

Dinosaur's spine   Cut 1 white 3 times as long as this

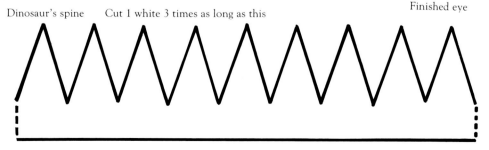

Baby's ball and cube

The ball is knitted in pastel colours which would grace any baby's crib, cot or pram, but for an older child or toddler why not try it in bolder colours with some embroidery. The cube is made from six knitted squares with letters of the alphabet and numbers knitted in.

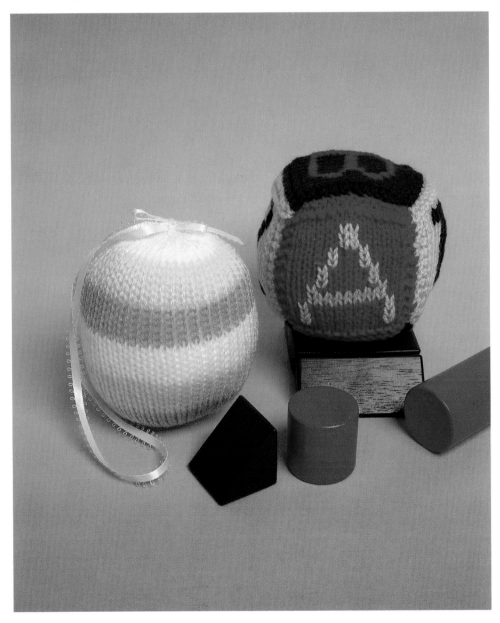

Materials

Baby's ball: Patons Knit 'n' Save DK: 1 (25g) ball each in white, pale blue and pink
Pair of 4mm (No 8) knitting needles
Washable polyester toy filling
1 yd (90cm) of narrow ribbon

Cube: Patons Knit 'n' Save DK: 1 (25g) ball each in royal, yellow and red
Pair of 4mm (No 8) knitting needles
Washable polyester toy filling

BABY'S BALL

Main piece (make 1)

Using white, cast on 7 sts and k 1 row.
Beg with a p row work in st st stripes of 6 rows white, 6 rows blue and 6 rows pink as follows:
Next row: (Inc in every st) to end: 14 sts.
K 1 row.
Next row: (Inc in every st) to end: 28 sts.
Beg with a k row, work 30 rows straight.
Next row: (K2 tog) 14 times.
P 1 row.
Next row: (K2 tog) 7 times. Cut off yarn, thread through remaining sts pull up and fasten off. Join seam, leaving an opening, fill and close opening. Run a thread round the cast on edge and pull up. Tie ribbon in a bow and sew to top of ball.

CUBE

The Square (make 6)

For each square, cast on 16 sts and k 3 rows.
Row 1: K.
Row 2: K2, p12, k2.
Repeat these 2 rows eight times more.
* K 3 rows and cast off. *
Work motifs from charts opposite as follows (charts show centre 12 stitches):
2 in red with "A" and "C".
2 in yellow with "1" and " 2".
2 in blue with "B" and "3".
For example for letter "C":
Cast on 16 sts and k 3 rows.
Row 1: K.
Row 2: K2, p5, then work 5 sts in contrast colour, p2, k2.
Continue until row 18 of motif has been completed. Work from * to *.

Finishing

Join all squares together following the diagram, leaving a small opening for filling. Fill softly and close the opening.

Sewing up cube

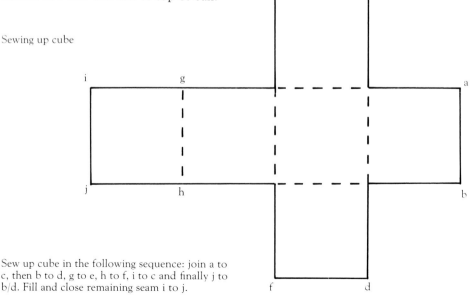

Sew up cube in the following sequence: join a to c, then b to d, g to e, h to f, i to c and finally j to b/d. Fill and close remaining seam i to j.

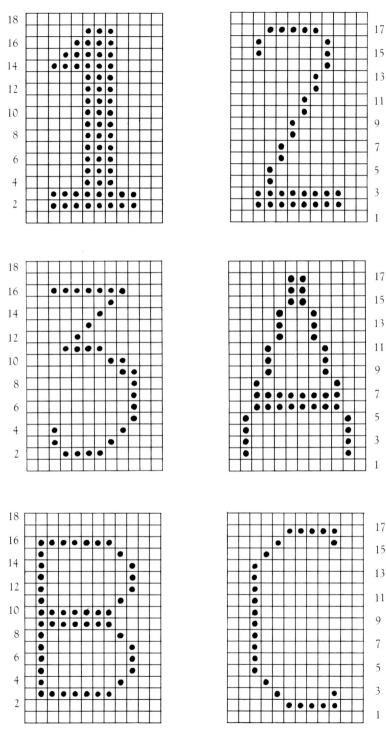

Baby's cube   Key: ☐ = main colour   ⦿ = contrast colours

Pet earthworm

Knitted in lime green, this pet is perfect for older children and even teenagers! All ready for his daily walkies with collar and lead, he'll strike a perfect pose in his diamond-studded neckwear!

Materials
Patons Knit 'n' Save DK: 1 (25g) ball in
  lime green; small amount of black
Pair of 4mm (No 8) knitting needles
20in (50cm) of fine wire
Washable polyester toy filling
15 diamante beads
2 buttons for eyes
1 yd (90cm) of gold chain

Body
Cast on 7 sts and work in st st as follows:
Inc 1 st each end of every 3rd row until
there are 21 sts, ending with a k row. Beg
with a p row, work 7 rows straight, then
inc 1 st each end of next row: 23 sts.
Work straight until work measures 17in
(43cm), ending with a p row.
Shape top: Next row: (K2 tog) 11 times,
k1.
P 1 row.
Next row: (K2 tog) 6 times. Cut off yarn,
thread through remaining sts and fasten
off. Join the seam, inserting the wire and
filling as you go.

Collar
Using black, cast on 30 sts and k 1 row.
Cast off. Sew on the beads, then put
collar on worm and join the seam.

Finishing
Sew on the buttons for the eyes, then
embroider a nose and mouth in black
yarn (see page 78). Sew the chain to the
collar. Bend to shape.

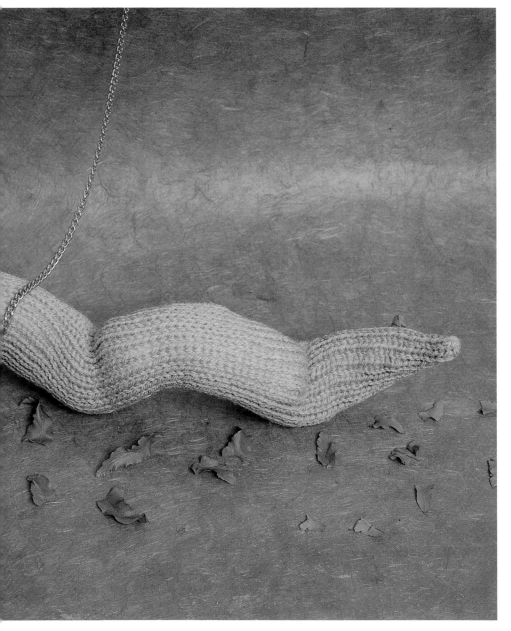

Spider cushion

The easiest and cheapest way to fill the spider is with a cushion pad and Hey Presto! he becomes a cushion. What child or discerning teenager could possibly do without one?

Materials
200g Patons Mohair in bright pink;
   1 (25g) ball Patons Knit 'n' Save DK in
   white; small amount of lime green
Pair each 5½mm (No 5) and 4mm (No 8)
   knitting needles
4in (10cm) square of black felt
Washable polyester toy filling
14in (36cm) zip
Round cushion pad approximately 14in
   (36cm) across

Tension
Tension is 16 sts and 20 rows to 4in
(10cm) over rev st st using 5½mm (No 5)
knitting needles

Body (make 2)
Using 5½mm knitting needles and pink,
cast on 16 sts. Work in rev st st
throughout. Beg with a p row, work 2
rows. Cast on 3 sts at the beg of the next
6 rows, then 2 sts at the beg of the next 4
rows. Inc 1 st each end of next and every
following alternate row until there are 56
sts, ending with a p row. Inc 1 st each
end of every following 4th row until
there are 60 sts. Work 9 rows straight, so
ending with a p row. Dec 1 st each end of
next and every following 4th row until 54
sts remain, then every following alternate
row until 42 sts remain, then cast off 2 sts
at beg of next 4 rows and 3 sts at beg of
next 6 rows. Work 1 row and cast off.

Legs (make 8)
Using 5½mm needles and pink, cast on 30
sts. Work in rev st st throughout. Beg
with a p row, work 4 rows.
Row 1: P13, p2 tog, p2 tog tbl, p13.
**Row 2 and every following alternate
row:** K.

Row 3: P12, p2 tog, p2 tog tbl, p12.
Row 5: P11, p2 tog, p2 tog tbl, p11.
Row 7: P10, p2 tog, p2 tog tbl, p10.
Beg with a k row, work 6½in (16cm) in rev
st st, ending with a k row. Cast on 16 sts
at beg of next 2 rows: 54 sts. Work 2¾in
(7cm), ending with a k row. Cast off.

Sole (make 8)
Using 5½mm needles and pink, cast on 4
sts and p 1 row. Beg with a k row,
continue in rev st st, inc 1 st each end of
next 3 rows: 10 sts. Work 7 rows
straight. Dec 1 st each end of next 3
rows. Cast off.

Eyes (make 2)
Using 4mm needles and white, cast on 8
sts and k 1 row. Work in st st
throughout.
Row 1: P1, inc in next 7 sts: 15 sts.
K 1 row.
Row 3: (P1, inc in next st) 7 times,
p1: 22 sts.
Work 10 rows in st st.
Next row: (K2 tog) 11 times.
P 1 row.
Next row: (K2 tog) 5 times, k1.
P 1 row. Cut off yarn and thread through
remaining sts. Pull up and fasten off. Join
seam and fill. Cut out 2 circles from felt
following the diagram and sew to top of
eyes.

Spider's eye
Cut 2 black

Nose (make 1)

Using 4mm needles and lime green, cast on 4 sts and k 1 row. Work in st st throughout.

Next row: (Inc in every st) to end: 8 sts. K 1 row.

Next row: (Inc in next st, p1) 4 times: 12 sts.

Work 4 rows in st st.

Next row: (K2 tog) 6 times. P 1 row.

Next row: (K2 tog) 3 times. Cut off yarn and thread through remaining sts, pull up and fasten off. Sew the seam, filling as you go, and sew to head.

Finishing

Sew seams of body, sewing in the zip at the same time. Join leg seams, then sew soles to ends of legs. Fill legs, then sew legs to sides of body. Cut out mouth shape from felt following the diagram and sew to head. Sew on eyes and nose. Insert the cushion pad.

Spider's mouth
Cut 1 black

Brainy bee

The brainy bee is a simple ball with colourful stripes and long bendy legs. He's on a piece of elastic so you can dangle him from the ceiling. Suitable for older children, he'll be an inspiration at homework time!

Materials

Patons Knit 'n' Save DK: 1 (25g) ball in black; 1 (25g) ball in yellow
Pair of 4mm (No 8) knitting needles

Washable polyester toy filling
11 pipe cleaners
1 half ball button and 2 flat black buttons
10in (25cm) of black elastic

Body (make 1)

Work in st st stripes of 4 rows black and 4 rows yellow throughout.

Cast on 11 sts and work 2 rows.

Next row: (Inc in every st) to end: 22 sts. P 1 row.

Next row: (Inc in every st) to end: 44 sts. Beg with a p row, work 25 rows.

Next row: (K2 tog) 22 times.

Next row: (P2 tog) 11 times. Cut off yarn and thread through remaining sts. Pull up and fasten off. Join seam, filling as you go. Run a gathering thread round cast on edge and pull up.

Head (make 1)

Using black, cast on 7 sts and k 1 row. Beg with a p row, work in st st as follows:

Next row: (Inc in every st) to end: 14 sts. K 1 row.

Next row: (Inc in every st) to end: 28 sts. K 1 row. Join on yellow.

Row 1: P10 black, 2 yellow, 4 black, 2 yellow, 10 black.

Row 2: K9 black, 4 yellow, 2 black, 4 yellow, 9 black.

Row 3: P8 black, 5 yellow, 2 black, 5 yellow, 8 black.

Row 4: K7 black, 14 yellow, 7 black.

Row 5: P7 black, 14 yellow, 7 black.

Rows 6 to 12: Repeat rows 4 and 5 three times, then row 4 again.

Row 13: As row 4 but p.

Row 14: As row 3 but k.

Row 15: As row 2 but p.

Row 16: As row 1 but in k.

Row 17: P with black. Cut off yellow.

Row 18: (K2 tog) 14 times.

Row 19: P.

Row 20: (K2 tog) 7 times.

Row 21: P. Cut off yarn and thread through remaining sts. Pull up and fasten off. Join seam, filling as you go. Sew to the body.

Finishing

Wings: (Make 4) Bind a pipe cleaner with black yarn, covering completely. Bend to shape following the diagram. Sew to the back of the body.

Legs: (Make 6) Bind 1 pipe cleaner in same way and bend following the diagram, sew to the body.

Antennae: Bind 1 pipe cleaner in same way, bend in half and roll ends slightly, then sew to top of head.

Embroider mouth and glasses (see diagram and page 78). Sew on half ball button for nose and the 2 flat buttons for eyes. Sew on elastic.

Wind yarn round a pipe cleaner

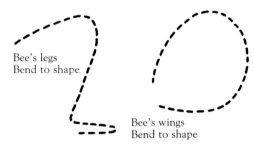

Bee's legs
Bend to shape

Bee's wings
Bend to shape

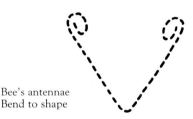

Bee's antennae
Bend to shape

Bee's face

THREE

Raggies and Glove Puppets

Hansel and Gretel

Hansel and Gretel are worked from the same basic pattern, just change the clothes and faces. And you can change them again to make another delightful fairytale couple.

HANSEL

Materials

Patons Knit 'n' Save DK: 1 (25g) ball each in white, red, beige, navy; small ball of rust for hair and oddments for embroidery
Pair of 4mm (No 8) knitting needles
Medium crochet hook
Washable polyester toy filling
2 buttons for shorts and 2 for sweater

Body and head (make 1)

Using white, cast on 44 sts and work 4in (10cm) in st st, working in stripes of 2 rows white and 2 rows red, ending with a p row. Join on beige.
Dec row: (K2 tog) 22 times: 22 sts.
P 1 row.
Next row: (Inc in every st) to end: 44 sts.
Beg with a p row, work 2¾in (7cm) in st st, ending with a p row.
Next row: (K2 tog) 22 times. P 1 row.
Next row: (K2 tog) 11 times. P 1 row.
Next row: (K2 tog) 5 times, k1.
Cut off yarn, thread through remaining sts, pull up and secure. Join back seam.
Fill body and head and join the lower seam. Run a thread round neck at dec row, pull up and secure. Wind the yarn round the neck a few times.

Legs (make 2)

* Using white, cast on 33 sts and k 1 row and p 1 row.
Row 1: K14, k2 tog tbl, k1, k2 tog, k14.
Row 2 and following alternate rows: P.
Row 3: K13, k2 tog tbl, k1, k2 tog, k13.
Row 5: K12, k2 tog tbl, k1, k2 tog, k12.
Row 7: K11, k2 tog tbl, k1, k2 tog, k11.
Row 9: K10, k2 tog tbl, k1, k2 tog, k10: 23 sts. *

Beg with a p row, work 6 rows in st st. K 3 rows. Join on beige and beg with a k row, work in st st until leg measures 7in (18cm) from cast on edge, ending with a p row. Cast off. Join centre back seam.

Sole (make 2)

Using white, cast on 5 sts and k 1 row. Beg with a p row, work in st st, inc 1 st each end of every row to 11 sts.
Work 8 rows straight.
Dec 1 st each end of every row until 5 sts remain. Cast off. Sew sole to leg, fill and sew to body.

Arms (make 2)

** Using white, cast on 6 sts and k 1 row. P 1 row. Continue in stripes of 2 rows red, 2 rows white, at the same time, inc 1 st each end of next 5 rows: 16 sts.
Mark each end of last row. **
Work 2¼in (6cm) straight, ending with a p row. Join on beige and work 4 rows.
Next row: (K2 tog) 8 times. P 1 row.
Next row: (K2 tog) 4 times.
Cut off yarn, thread through remaining sts, pull up and secure. Join seam. Fill and sew to body.

Ears (make 2)

Using beige, cast on 5 sts and k 2 rows. Work in garter stitch throughout. Dec 1 st each end of next row. K 1 row. K3 tog. Fasten off. Sew to head, folding sides round to form 'ears'.

Clothes
Boots (make 2)

*** Using navy, cast on 19 sts and k 1 row.
Row 1: Inc in first st, k8, M1, k1, M1, k8, inc in last st.

Row 2 and every following alternate row: K.
Row 3: Inc in first st, k9, M1, k3, M1, k9, inc in last st.
Row 5: Inc in first st, k10, M1, k5, M1, k10, inc in last st.
Row 7: Inc in first st, k11, M1, k7, M1, k11, inc in last st.
K 3 rows. ***
Row 1: K15, k2 tog tbl, k1, k2 tog, k15.

Row 2 and every following alternate row: K.
Row 3: K14, k2 tog tbl, k1, k2 tog, k14.
Row 5: K13, k2 tog tbl, k1, k2 tog, k13.
Row 7: K12, k2 tog tbl, k1, k2 tog, k12.
Cast off. Join seam. Make a 10in (25cm) crochet chain, tie in a bow; sew to front.

Shorts
Using navy, cast on 36 sts and k 3 rows.

47

Beg with a k row, work 2¼in (6cm) in st st, ending with a p row.
Cast on 2 sts at beg of next 2 rows: 40 sts. Continue in st st until work measures 5in (13cm) from the second cast on edges, ending with a k row.
Dec row: K6, (k2 tog) 14 times, k6.
**** Next row: (K1, p1) to end. Repeat this row 3 times more. ****
Cast off in rib. Work another piece in same way and sew front and back seams. Run a thread through ribbing and put on doll, pull up to fit.

Straps (make 2)
Using navy, cast on 44 sts and k 1 row. Cast off. Sew to shorts, crossing over at back and sewing buttons to front.

Collar
Using red, cast on 22 sts and k 1 row. Work in garter stitch. Now inc 1 st each end of next 7 rows. Cast off. Sew round neck. Sew the buttons down the front.

Beret
Using navy, cast on 50 sts and work as shorts from **** to ****.
Next row: (K1, inc in next st) 25 times: 75 sts.
Beg with a p row, work 5 rows st st.
Shape crown: Row 1: K4, (k2 tog, k3) 13 times, k2 tog, k4.
Row 2 and every following alternate row: P.
Row 3: K3, (k2 tog, k2) 13 times, k2 tog, k4.
Row 5: K3, (k2 tog, k1) 13 times, k2 tog, k3.
Row 7: K3, (k2 tog) 14 times, k2 tog, k2.
Row 9: (K2 tog) 9 times, k1.
Row 11: (K2 tog) 5 times. Cut off yarn, thread through remaining sts, pull and secure. Join seam. Make a small pompon in red and sew to top (see page 76).

Hair
Make a fringe in rust yarn (see page 77).

Features
Embroider eyes, mouth and nose (see page 78).

GRETEL

Materials
Patons Knit 'n' Save DK: 2 (25g) balls in pink; 1 (25g) ball in white; 2 (25g) balls in aqua; 2 (25g) balls in yellow; oddments for embroidery
Pair of 4mm (No 8) knitting needles
Washable polyester toy filling
4 buttons
20in (50cm) of narrow ribbon

Body and head
Work as for Hansel, using pink only to the dec row, then join on white and complete as for Hansel.

Legs
Work as Hansel from * to * but work in aqua. Then work in Spot Pattern as follows:
Row 1: K2 aqua, (1 yellow, 3 aqua) 5 times, 1 aqua.
Rows 2 to 5: Beg with a p row, work in st st with aqua.
Row 6: P2 aqua, (1 yellow, 3 aqua) 5 times, 1 aqua.
Rows 7 to 10: Beg with a k row work in st st with aqua.
Repeat these 10 rows for 7in (18cm), ending with a p row. Cast off.
Work soles as Hansel in aqua. Complete legs as Hansel.

Arms
Using pink, work as Hansel from ** to **, then work in st st for 2in (5cm), ending with a p row. Using yellow, work 2 rows, then using aqua work a further 2 rows. Cut off yellow and aqua, join on white and complete as for Hansel.

Skirt
Using pink, cast on 132 sts and k 1 row. Beg with a k row, work in st st stripes of 2 rows pink, 2 rows yellow, 2 rows aqua for 3¼in (8cm), ending with a p row.
Next row: (K3 tog) 44 times. K 4 rows. Cast off. Join back seam. Sew to body.

Collar
Using aqua, cast on 24 sts and k 1 row.

Cut off aqua, join on yellow and k 1 row and p 1 row.

Next row: (Inc in every st) to end: 48 sts. P 1 row.

Next row: (Inc in every st) to end: 96 sts. P 1 row and cast off loosely. Sew collar to neck. Sew 2 buttons down front of Gretel's body.

Shoes (make 2)

Using pink, work as Hansel's boots from *** to ***. Cast off.

Straps (make 2)

Using pink, cast on 18 sts and cast off.

Finishing

Join shoe seam. Sew strap to one side and button to other side.

Hair and features

Using yellow yarn, cut lengths and sew to centre of head, plait the yarn and tie on ribbons and work a row of loops across front for fringe. Work features as Hansel.

Comical clown

Colourful and comical, this clown will be loved by any child. Yet he is so easy and inexpensive to make. Cheap and cheerful, but lots of fun!

Materials

Patons Knit 'n' Save DK: 2 (25g) balls in yellow; 1 (25g) ball in lime; 1 (25g) ball in camel; 1 (25g) ball in royal; 3 (25g) balls in orange; small amount of white

Pair of 4mm (No 8) and 3¼mm (No 10) knitting needles

Washable polyester toy filling

2 buttons

Small amount of felt in black and white; 12½in × 1½in (32cm × 4cm) strip of orange felt

Pipe cleaner

20in (50cm) of narrow piping cord

Body and head

Work as for Hansel but work in stripes of 4 rows yellow and 4 rows lime to dec row. Join on camel; complete as Hansel.

Legs

Using yellow only, work as Wicked witch (see page 54).

Arms

Work as Hansel but work one in lime only and one in yellow only until work measures approximately 2¼in (6cm), ending with a p row. Then join on camel and work as for Hansel.

Trousers

Using orange, cast on 55 sts and k 3 rows. Beg with a k row, work 6in (15cm) in st st, ending with a p row.

Cast on 2 sts at beg of next 2 rows: 59 sts. Continue in st st until work measures 10in (25cm) from the beginning, ending with a k row.

Dec row: (P2 tog) 29 times, p1.

K 3 rows and cast off. Work another piece in same way.

Sew front and back seams. Embroider flowers using lazy daisy stitch and French knots, work 2 leaves as straight lines in green (see page 78).

Straps (make 2)

Using orange, cast on 38 sts and k 4 rows. Cast off. Sew one edge to back, cross over and sew to front with buttons.

Hat

Using royal, cast on 55 sts and work 20 rows in st st.

Shape top: Row 1: K1, (k2 tog, k1) 18 times.

Row 2 and every following alternate row: P.

Row 3: K1, (k2 tog, k1) 12 times.

Row 5: K1, (k2 tog, k1) 8 times.

Row 7: K1, (k2 tog) 8 times.

Row 8: (P2 tog) 4 times, p1. Cut off yarn, thread through remaining sts, pull up and sew seam, reversing last 8 rows.

Fill hat. Roll back first 8 rows and sew down. Sew to head.

Flower

Cut out shapes from felt following the diagram on page 52. Cover a pipe cleaner with lime yarn (see page 43), sew to back of flower then sew flower to hat.

Nose

Using 3¼mm needles and red, cast on 3 sts and k 1 row.

Beg with a p row, continue in st st as follows:

Row 1: (Inc in every st) to end.

K 1 row.

Row 3: (Inc in every st) to end.

Work 2 rows.

Row 6: (K2 tog) 6 times.

P 1 row.

Row 8: (K2 tog) 3 times. Cut off yarn, thread through remaining sts, pull up and sew seam. Sew to face, filling lightly.

Dickie bow

Using white, cast on 36 sts and work 10 rows st st. Cast off. Join short seam, gather centre, pull up and wind yarn round the centre. Embroider dots in orange (see page 78) and sew to neck.

Shoes

Top: Using yellow, cast on 4 sts and k 1 row. Continue in garter stitch, inc 1 st each end of next 3 rows, then following 2 alternate rows.

Work 3 rows, then inc 1 st each end of next row.

Repeat the last 4 rows once more.

K 6 rows, then dec 1 st each end of next and every following 4th row until 10 sts remain.

Work 1 row, then dec 1 st each end of next row. Cast off, dec 1 st each end. Work another shoe in the same way but work in lime.

Sole: Work as top in lime. Work another sole in yellow.

Bows (make 2)

Using white, cast on 18 sts and k 6 rows. Complete as for dickie bow. Sew to top of shoe.

Piping

Cut the strip of felt in half lengthways. Insert piping, fold over felt and sew to sole through the 2 thicknesses. Sew sole to top leaving an opening (see diagrams). Fill, then close opening. Sew to bottom of legs.

Features

Cut out 2 circles from felt following the diagram for eyes and sew to face. Embroider mouth (see page 78). Work loops in yellow round top of head (see page 77).

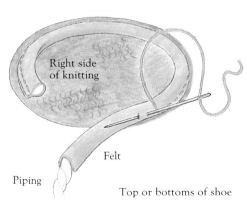

Right side of knitting

Felt

Piping

Top or bottoms of shoe

Sew through all thicknesses

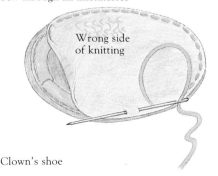

Wrong side of knitting

Clown's shoe

Flower
Cut out petals in white, centre in orange

Clown's eye
Cut 2 black

Flower centre

Wicked witch

This wicked witch is all you need with Hansel and Gretel to recreate the famous fairy tale. The witch's warts and pets add the finishing touches. This witch is suitable for older children.

Materials

Patons Knit 'n' Save DK: 5 (25g) balls in black; 1 (25g) ball each in lime green and red; small amount of yellow for embroidery

Pair each of 4mm (No 8) and 3¼mm (No 10) knitting needles

Washable polyester toy filling

18¾ × 1¼in (48 × 3cm) of black felt; 12in (30cm) square of lime green felt

2 pipe cleaners

Body and head

Using black, work as Hansel to dec row. Cut off black, join on lime and complete as for Hansel.

Legs (make 2)

Using red, cast on 23 sts and work 4 rows in st st. Join on black and work in stripes of 2 rows black, 2 rows red for 8¾in (22cm), ending with a p row. Cast off. Join seam, fill and sew to body.

Arms

Work as Hansel from ** to ** in black. Work 2¼in (6cm) straight, ending with a p row. Cut off black and join on lime and complete as Hansel.

Nose

Using 3¼mm needles and lime, cast on 7 sts and p 1 row. Continue in rev st st, dec 1 st each end of next and following alternate row. K 1 row. P3 tog and fasten off. Sew seam and sew to face. Embroider eyes, mouth and warts (see diagram and page 78).

Skirt

Using black, cast on 88 sts and k 1 row. Beg with a k row work 5¼in (13cm) in st st, ending with a k row.

Next row: (P2 tog) 44 times. Cast off. Join seam and sew to waist. Cut a length of black felt approximately 1¼in (3cm) wide, cut into a zig zag and sew to bottom of skirt.

Cape

Using black, cast on 132 sts and k 3 rows.

Row 1: K.

Row 2: K2, p to last 2 sts, k2.

Repeat these 2 rows once more.

Next row: K5, (k2 tog, k4) 20 times, k2 tog, k5.

Repeat rows 2 and 1 in that order seven times more, then work row 2 once more.

Next row: K5, (k2 tog, k3) 20 times, k2 tog, k4.

Repeat rows 2 and 1 seven times more, then row 2 once more.

Next row: K4, (k2 tog, k2) 20 times, k2 tog, k4.

Repeat rows 2 and 1 seven times more.

Next row: K4, (k2 tog, k1) 20 times, k2 tog, k3.

Work row 2, row 1 and row 2.

Next row: K2, (k2 tog) 22 times, k2.

Collar: K 1 row.

Next row: K2, inc in next st, p to last 3 sts, inc in next st, k2.

Next row: K2, inc in next st, k to last 3 sts, inc in next st, k2.

Repeat last 2 rows 4 times more. Cast off knitwise. Embroider stars in yellow (see diagram).

Witch's face

Stars on Witch's cape
Work in straight lines

Hat

Using black, cast on 50 sts and work 6 rows in st st.

Row 1: (Skp, k21, k2 tog) twice.
Row 2: P.
Row 3: K.
Row 4: P.
Row 5: (Skp, k19, k2 tog) twice.
Rows 6 to 8: As rows 2 to 4.
Continue to dec in this way on next and every following 4th row until 14 sts remain, then every following alternate row until 6 sts remain.
Work 3 rows straight.
Cut off yarn, thread through remaining sts and fasten off. Join seam.

Brim

Using black, cast on 50 sts and k 4 rows.
Next row: (K1, inc in next st) 25 times.
K 3 rows.
Next row: (K2, inc in next st) 25 times.
K 3 rows.
Next row: (K3, inc in next st) 25 times.
K 1 row and cast off loosely. Join short seam. Sew to hat.

Hair and features

Cut lengths of red yarn and sew to sides of head. Cut through loops but leave it untidy (see page 77). Sew on the hat. Embroider face as shown in diagram (see page 78 for embroidery stitches).

Shoes

Following the diagram, cut out shapes from green felt. Join the seams on the right side. Insert pipe cleaners into the toe before filling. Cut a length of felt approximately ½in × 5in (1cm × 12cm), cut into a zig zag and sew to top of each shoe.

Ladybird

Using 3¼mm needles and red, cast on 3 sts and k 1 row. Work in st st throughout.
Next row: (Inc in every st) to end.
K 1 row.
Next row: (Inc in every st) to end.
Work 3 rows straight.
Cut off red, join on black.
Next row: (P2 tog) 6 times. K 1 row.
Next row: (P2 tog) 3 times.
Cut off yarn, thread through remaining sts and fasten off. Join seam. Embroider dots in black (see page 78). Sew to dress or hat.

Worm

Using 3¼mm needles and lime, cast on 20 sts. Cast off. Embroider eye (see page 78) and sew to dress or hat.

Spider

Work body as ladybird but use red throughout. Embroider eyes (see page 78) and legs.

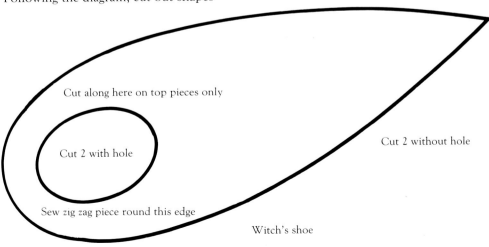

Cut along here on top pieces only

Cut 2 with hole

Cut 2 without hole

Sew zig zag piece round this edge

Witch's shoe

Animal glove puppets

A cat, a rabbit and a mouse – all from one pattern! The variations are endless – add a trunk and bigger ears for an elephant or spots for a leopard. Whichever you choose, children of all ages will have hours of fun with these puppet playmates.

Materials
Cat: Patons Knit 'n' Save DK: 1 (25g) ball each in black and white
Pair of 4mm (No 8) knitting needles
Pipe cleaner
4in (10cm) square of black felt; small amounts of green and pink felt

Mouse: Patons Knit 'n' Save DK: 1 (25g) ball in blue; oddments of black for embroidery
Pair of 4mm (No 8) knitting needles
6in (15cm) square of pink felt; small amount of brown felt
2 buttons for eyes

Rabbit: Patons Knit 'n' Save DK: 1 (25g) ball in pink; small amount of white for tail; oddments of black for embroidery
Pair of 4mm (No 8) knitting needles
6in (15cm) square of white felt; small amount of brown felt
2 buttons for eyes

CAT

Work basic body and head (below), casting on with black and working in st st stripes of 4 rows black, 4 rows white throughout.

Basic body and head (make 2)
Cast on 35 sts and k 3 rows.
Beg with a k row, work 5in (13cm) in st st, ending with a p row.
Divide for top: Next row: K9, turn and leave remaining sts on a spare needle.
* Work 1½in (3.5cm) in st st, ending with a p row. Dec 1 st each end of next and

following alternate row: 5 sts.
Cast off dec 1 st each end. *
With right side facing, join on yarn and k 17, turn and leave remaining sts on a spare needle.
Work 2in (5cm) in st st, ending with a p row. Dec 1 st each end of next and following 2 alternate rows, then every row until 7 sts remain.
Cast off dec 1 st each end.
With right side facing, join on yarn and k remaining 9 sts. Work from * to * once.
Join seams.

Tail
Using black, cast on 15 sts and work 2¼in (6cm) in st st, ending with a p row.
Using white, work 3 rows. Dec 1 st each end of next 6 rows. P 3 tog and fasten off.
Fold in half lengthways and join seam.
Insert pipe cleaner, curl and sew to body.

Ears
Cut out shapes from black felt following the diagram. Sew seams on right side and sew to head.

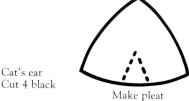

Cat's ear
Cut 4 black

Make pleat

Features
Cut out 2 eye shapes from green felt following the diagram on page 58 and sew to face. Sew a line of black yarn across

centre and embroider a mouth. Cut out nose shape from pink felt and sew to face.

Cat's eye
Cut 2 green

Line for yarn

Nose (for any glove puppet)

MOUSE

Work main body in blue as for cat.

Tail
Cut out shapes from pink felt following the diagram, sew seam on right side and sew to body.

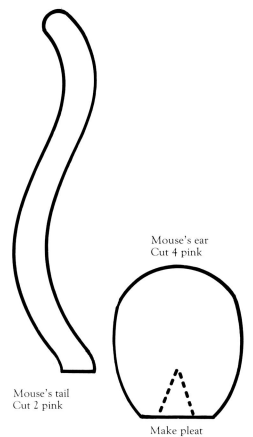

Mouse's ear
Cut 4 pink

Mouse's tail
Cut 2 pink

Make pleat

Ears
Cut out shapes from pink felt following the diagram. Sew seams on right side and sew to head.

Features
Sew on buttons for eyes. Cut out nose shape from felt following the diagram and sew to face. Embroider mouth in black yarn (see page 79).

RABBIT

Work main body in pink as for cat.

Tail
Make a small pompon in white (see page 76) and sew to back.

Ears
Cut out shapes from white felt following the diagram. Sew seams on right side and sew to head.

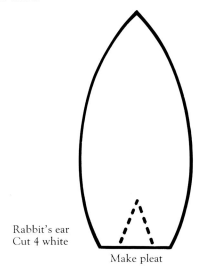

Rabbit's ear
Cut 4 white

Make pleat

Features
Sew on buttons for eyes. Cut out nose shape from brown felt following the diagram and sew to face.
Embroider mouth in black yarn (see page 79).

Santa with a present

Santa is all ready to bring the presents! And if not given as a present himself, he will look just as good as a festive table decoration.

Materials

Patons Knit 'n' Save DK: 1 (25g) ball in red, camel, black, white and yellow; oddments for embroidery
Pair of 4mm (No 8) knitting needles
Washable polyester toy filling
16in (40cm) of festive ribbon

Body

Using red, cast on 11 sts and k 1 row and p 1 row. Work in st st throughout.
Row 1: (Inc in every st) to end: 22 sts.
P 1 row.
Row 3: (Inc in every st) to end: 44 sts.
Beg with a p row, work 25 rows in st st.
Next row: (K2 tog) 22 times.
Next row: (P2tog) 11 times.
Cut off yarn, thread through remaining sts, pull up and fasten off, join seam, leaving an opening, fill and close the seam. Run a gathering thread round cast on edge and pull up.

Head

Using camel, cast on 7 sts, k 1 row and p 1 row. Work in st st throughout.
Row 1: (Inc in every st) to end: 14 sts.
P 1 row.
Row 3: (Inc in every st) to end: 28 sts.
Beg with a p row, work 15 rows in st st.
Next row: (K2 tog) 14 times.
Next row: (P2 tog) 7 times.
Cut off yarn, thread through remaining sts, pull up and fasten off. Join seam, leaving an opening, fill and close seam. Run a thread through edge as for body.

Legs (make 2)

Using black, cast on 26 sts, k 1 row and p 1 row.
Row 1: K11, k2 tog, skp, k11.
P 1 row.

Row 3: K10, k2 tog, skp, k10.
P 1 row.
Row 5: K9, k2 tog, skp, k9.
Beg with a p row, work 5 rows in st st.
Cut off black, join on white and k 4 rows.
Cut off white, join on red and beg with a k row, work 4 rows in st st, then cast off.

Sole

Using black, cast on 4 sts and k 1 row.
Beg with a k row, work in st st, inc 1 st each end of next 2 rows. Work 7 rows straight. Dec 1 st each end of next 2 rows, then cast off.
Sew the leg seam, sew sole to base of leg, fill and sew legs to the body.

Arms (make 2)

Using red, cast on 12 sts and work 18 rows in st st. Join on white and k 4 rows.
Using red, beg with a k row and work 6 rows in st st.
Next row: (K2 tog) 6 times.
Cut off yarn, thread through remaining sts, pull up and fasten off, then join seam.
Fill and sew to body.

Hood (make 1)

Using white, cast on 35 sts and k 3 rows.
Join on red and beg with a k row, work 2in (5cm) in st st, ending with a p row.
Cast off. Join the back seam. Catch down cast on edge of hood to head.

Edgings

Waist: Using white, cast on 54 sts and k 2 rows. Cast off.
Front: Using white, cast on 14 sts and k 2 rows. Cast off.
Sew front edging in place from neck downwards, then sew waist in place, joining seam at back.

Features

Work eyes, eyebrows, nose and mouth
(see diagram and page 78).
Beard: Work a row of loops in white
(see page 77).

Parcel

Using yellow, cast on 13 sts and k 44
rows. Cast off. Fold in half and sew the
seam. Tie on the ribbon and make a bow
in the front. Sew hands round the parcel.

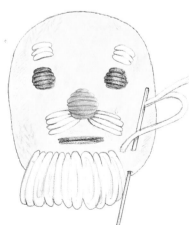

Santa's face
Work loops in white

Santa's elf

Santa always needs his helpers for his busiest time of the year and this elf really is a fine festive fellow in his splendid green coat and hat. If making him for a small child, do not use the bell or pipe cleaners.

Materials

Patons Knit 'n' Save DK: 1 (25g) balls in green; small amounts of camel, black, pink and white
Pair of 4mm (No 8) knitting needles
Washable polyester toy filling
2 pipe cleaners
7in (18cm) square of red felt
Small toy bell (optional)

Body and head

Using green, cast on 32 sts and work 22 rows in st st.
Cut off green, join on camel.
Dec row: (K2 tog) 16 times: 16 sts.
Next row: P2, inc in next 12 sts, p2: 28 sts.
Work 16 rows in st st.
Next row: (K2 tog) 14 times.
Next row: (P2 tog) 7 times.
Cut off yarn, thread through remaining sts, pull up and fasten off, join seams, leaving an opening, fill and close the seam. Run a thread round the dec row at neck, pull up and secure.

Arms (make 2)

Work as for Angel on page 70 but use green instead of white and camel instead of pink. Join seam, fill and sew to body.

Legs (make 2)

Using green, cast on 12 sts and work 30 rows in st st. Cast off. Join seam, fill and sew to body.

Shoes (make 2)

Using green, cast on 5 sts and k 1 row.
Beg with a p row, work in st st, inc 1 st each end of every row until there are 11 sts. Work 17 rows straight. Dec 1 st each end of next and every following 4th row until 3 sts remain, ending with a p row. K 1 row and p 1 row. K3 tog and fasten off. Join seams, filling as you go with the pipe cleaner down the centre. Curl fronts. Cut out a rectangle in felt 3½in × ½in (8.5cm × 1cm) and zig zag the edge. Sew to top of shoe then sew shoe to ends of legs.

Collar (make 1)

Using green, cast on 25 sts.
Next row: K, inc 3 sts evenly across.
Repeat this row 3 times more. Cast off.
Sew to neck.

Jacket and belt (make 1)

Using green, cast on 46 sts and k 1 row.
Beg with a k row, work 10 rows in st st.
Join on white and k 3 rows. Cast off. Join back seam and sew to waist of body.
Embroider buckle in black (see diagram and page 78).

Elf's buckle
Work lines in black yarn

64

Hood

Using green, cast on 38 sts and work 2 rows in st st.

Row 1: (Skp, k15, k2 tog) twice.

Rows 2 to 4: Beg with a p row work in st st.

Row 5: (Skp, k13, k2 tog) twice.

Rows 6, 7 and 8: As rows 2, 3 and 4. Work in this way, dec on next and every following 4th row until 18 sts remain, ending with a p row. Dec 1 st as before on next and every following alternate row until 6 sts remain, ending with a k row.

Next row: (P2 tog) 3 times.

Cut off yarn, thread through remaining sts, pull up and fasten off, join seam. Cut out a rectangle in felt 7in × ½in (18cm × 1cm), zig zag the edge and sew to hat. Work in the same way for the cuffs. Sew the hat to the head then sew on the bell (if used).

Features

Embroider eyes, nose and mouth (see page 78).

Beard: Work a row of loops in white yarn (see page 77).

Christmas penguin

Chubby, cute and cuddly, this penguin is looking for a warm home this Christmas. What child could resist him?

Materials
Patons Knit 'n' Save DK: 1 (25g) ball each in white and black; small amount of red for bow tie
Pair of 4mm (No 8) knitting needles
Washable polyester toy filling
6in (15cm) square of orange felt; 4in (10cm) square of yellow felt; small amount of black felt or 2 buttons for eyes

Body and head
Using white, cast on 6 sts, k 1 row and p 1 row.
Row 1: (Inc in every st) to end: 12 sts.
P 1 row.
Row 3: (Inc in every st) to end: 24 sts.
Beg with a p row, work 29 rows in st st.
Next row: K, dec 3 sts evenly across: 21 sts.
Beg with a p row, work 5 rows in st st.
Work in 2 colours as follows:
Row 1: K10 white, 1 black, 10 white.
Row 2: P10 white, 1 black, 10 white.
Row 3: Using white skp, k8, k1 black, k8 white, k2 tog.
Row 4: P8 white, 3 black, 8 white.
Row 5: Using white skp, k5, k5 black, k5 white, k2 tog.
Row 6: P3 white, 11 black, 3 white. Cut off white.
Row 7: Skp, k to last 2 sts, k2 tog.
Row 8: P.
Cast off 2 sts at beg of next 4 rows, then cast off. Make another piece in the same way but all in black. Join the seams, leaving an opening, fill and close seam.

Wings (make 2)
Using black, cast on 17 sts and work 10 rows in st st. Dec 1 st each end of next and every following alternate row until 5 sts remain. Cast off, dec 1 st each end. Fold in half, sew seam, then sew to body.

Tail (make 1)
Using black, cast on 12 sts and k 4 rows. Continue in garter stitch, dec 1 st each end of every row until 2 sts remain. K2 tog and fasten off. Sew to base.

Finishing
Cut out feet and beak shapes from orange and yellow felt following the diagrams. Join beak and feet seams on

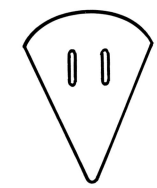

Penguin's beak
Cut 2 yellow
Work lines in black yarn

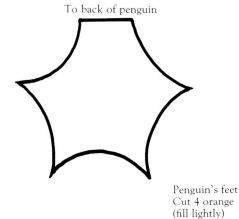

To back of penguin

Penguin's feet
Cut 4 orange
(fill lightly)

right side, filling lightly, and sew beak to face and feet to base. Work 2 straight lines in black yarn down beak.

Bow tie: Using red, cast on 8 sts and k 8 rows. Cast off. Wrap yarn round centre and pull up; fasten off. **For tie:** Using red, cast on 50 sts and p 1 row. Cast off. Place tie round the neck and sew ends. Sew bow over tie.

Cut out 2 small circles in black felt for eyes and sew or glue to face, or use 2 small shiny black buttons.

Snowman with bobble hat

Dreaming of a White Christmas and ready for the winter in his warm bobble hat and scarf. He really makes the festive scene.

Materials
Patons Knit 'n' Save DK: 1 (25g) ball each in white, green and red; small amounts of orange and black
Pair each of 4mm (No 8) and 3¼ mm (No 10) knitting needles
Washable polyester toy filling
2 buttons

Body
Using 4mm needles and white, cast on 12 sts and work 2 rows in st st. Work in st st throughout.
Row 1: (Inc in every st) to end: 24 sts.
P 1 row.
Next row: (Inc in every st) to end: 48 sts.
Beg with a p row, work 29 rows in st st.
Next row: (K2 tog) 24 times.
P 1 row.
Next row: (K2 tog) 12 times.
Cut off yarn and thread through remaining sts, pull up and sew seam, leaving an opening, fill and close opening. Run a thread round cast on edge and pull up.

Head
Work as head of Santa on page 62 in white.

Scarf
Using green, cast on 62 sts and work 6 rows in st st. Cast off. Gather each end. Make 2 small pompons in red and sew to ends (see page 76).

Hat
Using red, cast on 42 sts and work 4 rows in k1, p1 rib.
Work 12 rows in st st.
Next row: (K2 tog) 21 times.
P 1 row.
Next row: (K2 tog) 10 times, k1.
P 1 row.

Next row: (K2 tog) 5 times, k1.
Cut off yarn, thread through remaining sts, pull up and join seam. Make a small pompon in green and sew to top (see page 76).

Nose
Using 3¼mm needles and orange, cast on 9 sts and p 1 row and k 1 row. Beg with a p row, work in rev st st, dec 1 st each end of next and every following alternate row until 3 sts remain. K3 tog and fasten off. Join seam and sew to face.

Features
Embroider eyes and mouth in black yarn (see page 78). Sew buttons down front.

Angel for the tree

Charming enough to grace the top of any tree, but she could easily become any doll you choose – knit a brightly coloured short dress and give her plaits, or add short hair for an angelic choir-boy.

Materials

Patons Knit 'n' Save DK: 1 (25g) ball each in white, pink and yellow; small amounts of brown and darker pink for embroidery
Pair of 4mm (No 8) knitting needles
Washable polyester toy filling
12in (30cm) of gold ribbon
6in (15cm) square of white felt for wings
12in (30cm) of gold wire

Body and head

Using white, cast on 24 sts and work 24 rows in st st.
Dec row: (K2 tog) 12 times: 12 sts.
P 1 row. Cut off white, join on pink.
Inc row: (Inc in every st) to end: 24 sts.
Beg with a p row, work 9 rows in st st.
Shape top: Next row: (K2 tog) 12 times.
P 1 row.
Next row: (K2 tog) 6 times.
Cut off yarn, thread through remaining sts, pull up and join seam.
Fill and close the bottom seam. Sew a line for 1½in (4cm) through all thicknesses from the cast on edge to form legs. Wind yarn round the dec row at neck and pull up. Fasten off securely.

Arms

Using white, cast on 3 sts and k 1 row.
Beg with a p row, work in st st, inc 1 st each end of next and following 2 alternate rows: 9 sts. Beg with a p row, work 9 rows in st st. Cut off white, join on pink and work 4 rows.
Dec row: (K2 tog) 4 times, k1.
Cut off yarn, thread through remaining sts, pull up and join seam.
Fill and sew to body, joining hands together at front.

Skirt

Using white, cast on 60 sts and k 1 row.
Beg with a k row, work 16 rows in st st.
Dec row: (K2 tog) 30 times. Cast off knitwise. Join seam and sew to waist of body. Sew ribbon to bottom of dress.

Finishing

Cut out wings following diagram. Join seams on right side and sew to back of body along the fold line.

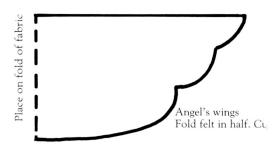

Place on fold of fabric

Angel's wings
Fold felt in half. Cu

Work hair in yellow and embroider eyes, nose and mouth (see pages 77 and 78). Make halo using wire, following the diagram.

Wind the yarn round the angel's head from front to back, securing it through the tacking stitch each time

70

Shape 1

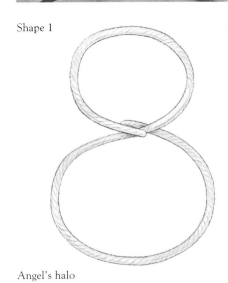

Shape 2

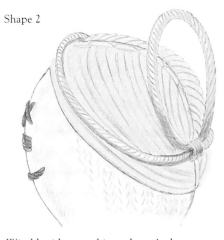

Angel's halo

Wind braid or cord into shape 1, then secure
join at back with thick or doubled length of
cotton into shape 2

Better Techniques

Read this chapter before you start as it demonstrates the various techniques you will need to master to enable you to begin knitting the toys featured in this book.

Equipment

You do not have to buy a great deal of expensive equipment to begin knitting toys, so it is a popular craft for children to take up. Buy good quality branded name products if possible and always buy enough of the same dye lot to complete your work. Dye lots can differ greatly from one batch to the next so any change will be very obvious.

The main tools you will require are:
Needles – these come in various lengths and are usually made from plastic, steel and bamboo (the bamboo needles are especially good for arthritic knitters). Below is a conversion table:

Knitting needle sizes

Metric	(old sizes)	American
3¼mm	10	3
3¾mm	9	4
4mm	8	5
4½mm	7	6
5mm	6	7
5½mm	5	8
6mm	4	9
6½mm	3	10

Cable needles are short double pointed needles used in Aran patterns.

Circular needles are used for working in 'rounds' such as yokes or wherever a join or seam is not wanted. They are available in various lengths and sizes.
Row counter – this neat little device fits on to the end of your needle so you can count the number of rows you have done, very useful when working in lace.
Pins – choose pins with large heads, small headed pins will slip through the knitting, be very careful not to leave any pins in the toys once they are finished.
Darning needles – choose needles with sharp points and large eyes as the yarn can then be threaded easily.
Sharp scissors and a good quality **tape measure**.

Casting on

The best method of casting on is called cable or 2 needle method. It gives a firm, neat edge.

First make a slip knot and place it on the left hand needle, leaving a long end for sewing up with. Insert the point of the right hand needle into the front of this loop, wind yarn round needle, pull

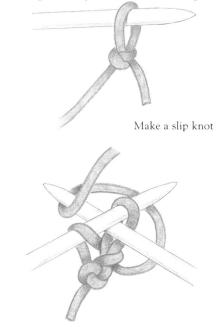

Make a slip knot

Insert needle between these two stitches, wind yarn round and pull loop through

Repeat until you have the stated number of stitches

To knit a stitch

the loop through and place it on the left hand needle.

Now insert point of the needle between these two stitches, wind yarn round and pull the loop through, place it on the left hand needle. Repeat this procedure until you have the stated number of stitches.

Casting off

The best and easiest method of casting off is to also use 2 needles.

On knit rows, knit the first stitch as usual, knit the second stitch and with the point of the left hand needle pass the first stitch over the second stitch and off the needle. Repeat this procedure to the end. When the last stitch has been worked and you only have one stitch left on the needle, cut off the yarn leaving a long end for sewing up with, pull it through the last stitch to fasten off.

On purl rows, work exactly as on knit rows but purl each stitch.

To cast off in rib, knit over a knit stitch, take the yarn to the front and purl the next stitch, slipping the knit stitch over it, repeat these procedures all along the row.

To knit

After casting on work back across the loops as follows:
With the yarn at the back and with the point of the right hand needle, insert into the last stitch cast on from the front to the back.

Wind yarn round the point of the right hand needle, pull the loop through on to the right hand needle, slipping the cast on stitch off the needle. Repeat to the end.

To purl

As with the knit stitch, work back across the cast on stitches as follows:
With the yarn at the front and with the point of the right hand needle, insert into the last stitch cast on from the back to the front.

Wind yarn round the point of the right hand needle and pull the loop through on to the right hand needle, slipping the cast on stitch off the needle. Repeat to the end.

To purl a stitch

Garter stitch

In garter stitch, every stitch and every row is knitted.

Stocking stitch

One row (the first after casting on) is knitted, the next row is purled.

Reversed stocking stitch

One row (the first after casting on) is purled, the next row is knitted.

Ribbing

This can be any combination of stitches beginning with one knit and one purl.

Colour change

When working in blocks or 'areas' of colour, it is much easier to use small balls of yarn than to strand across: when the stated number of stitches have been worked in one colour, leave this colour at the back of the knitting, pick up the next colour and twist the two yarns round each other so preventing a hole forming. Do this on both the right and wrong sides of the work.

To change colour

Tension

This is the most important but always the most overlooked part of knitting. To check your tension first cast on 28 stitches using a pair of 4mm (No 8) needles and work 36 rows in stocking stitch, then cast off. Count out 22 stitches and 30 rows, measure, and if the square measures MORE than 4in (10cm) your tension is LOOSE and you will need to try again using a needle one size smaller, eg 3¾mm (No 9), and so on until the square measures correctly. If the square measures LESS than 4in (10cm) your tension is TIGHT and you will need to try again using a needle one size bigger, eg 4½mm (No 7), and so on until the square measures correctly.

Simple decrease and increase

To decrease one stitch (sloping to the left), work "skp" – slip the first stitch, knit the next stitch and pass the slipped stitch over it, or k2 tog tbl – insert the needle into both stitches from front to back.

To decrease one stitch (sloping to the right), work k2 tog – knit the next two stitches together by inserting the needle into both stitches at the same time.

Work purl decreases as follows: to decrease one stitch (sloping to the left), work p2 tog tbl – insert the needle into

both stitches from back to front.

To decrease one stitch (sloping to the right), work p2 tog – as k2 tog but purl the stitches.

To increase at either end of a row, knit or purl the stitch in the usual way but leave the stitch on the needle, then knit or purl the same stitch again but work into the back of the stitch this time and slip it off the needle.

To make one (M1), with the point of the needle, pick up the horizontal loop that lies between the stitch just worked and the next stitch on the needle, place it on the left hand needle, then knit or purl into the back of it.

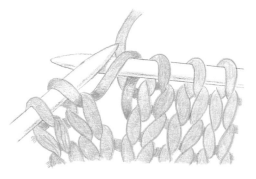

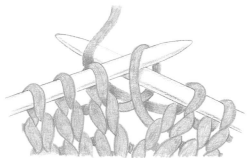

To make a stitch

Charts

To work from a chart in stocking stitch always read the chart from right to left beginning at the bottom right hand corner. Strand the yarns not being used loosely across the back of the work, linking in every 4 or 5 stitches. Refer to 'colour change' for working in large areas. Right side (odd numbered knit rows) are worked from right to left and wrong side (even numbered purl rows) are worked from left to right.

Sewing up

This is probably the most difficult part for knitters after finishing the work. The best methods of sewing up, especially toys, are back stitching, oversewing and the 'invisible method' or ladder stitch.

Always use a smooth similar colour yarn for sewing up, slubs are very difficult and can break.

Back stitching: Use this seam when a firm edge is required or when there is a lot of shaping and the edges need to be defined.

To back stitch

Place the knitting with right sides together and begin at the right hand side. Working from right to left bring the needle to the front, take it to the back across one stitch, then into the front again across one stitch.

Oversewing or flat stitching: This creates a very flat seam but is not as neat on the right side as back stitch or invisible seaming.

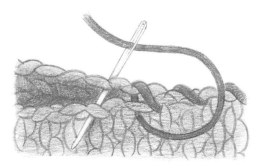

To oversew

Place the knitting with right sides together and begin at the right hand side. Working from right to left bring the needle from the back to the front spacing across one stitch to the end. Be careful not to pull the seam tightly when oversewing.

Invisible seaming (sometimes called ladder stitch): Used when a very neat seam is required.

Place the edges side by side with the right side of the work facing you. Begin at the lower edge and bring the needle up between the first and second stitches on the right hand side of the seam. Take the needle across to the left side and repeat. After about 4 or 5 stitches, pull up carefully to close the seam.

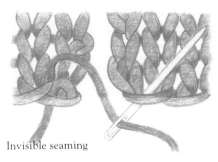

Invisible seaming

Cabling

The cable used for knitting the coat for the Cosy sheep in Chapter One on page 13 is a very simple 4 stitch cable (see the instructions below), but any combination of stitches can be used.

Across the next 4 stitches work as follows:

Slip the first 2 stitches on to the cable needle being careful not to twist the stitches and leave the cable needle at either the back or the front of the knitting.

Knit the next 2 stitches in the usual way, then knit the 2 stitches on the cable needle, knit the first stitch that was slipped then the second, ie work from right to left.

Special techniques

Pompons: These can be used as a fun form of decoration and are so easy to make, a child could do one.

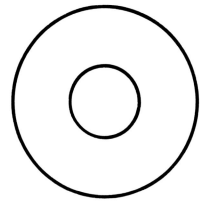

Actual size of pompon card   Cut 2

Pull card apart and tie centre

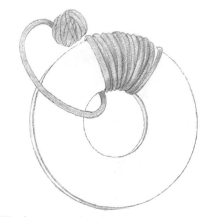

Wind yarn round card

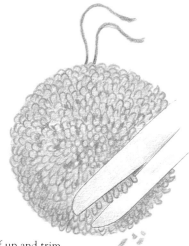

Fluff up and trim

Cut out 2 cardboard circles following the diagram for the size of pompon used in this book. Place the 2 circles together and wind the yarn evenly round the card.

When the hole is full, cut off the yarn, then cut through the layers being careful not to cut the card. Ease the card apart and, using a length of yarn, tie the centre very firmly. Pull the card pieces completely apart, fluff up the surface and trim.

Plaits: These are used for hair but can also be used for trimming.

Cut strands two-thirds longer than the length needed and divide into 3 equal parts. Fold each piece over into a plait. Tie the end of the plait securely with yarn or ribbon.

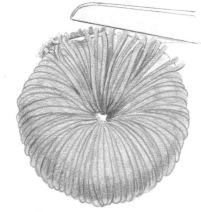

Cut strands

Tassels: These are very decorative and so easy to do.

Decide how long your tassel needs to be and cut out one piece of card this length.

Wind the yarn round the card until it is the thickness you want, cut it across, secure the strands together and wind the yarn round. Trim the ends.

Wind yarn round

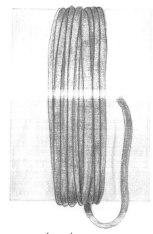

Wind yarn round card

Fringing and looping: These can be used for hair, beards, etc.

For hair, first mark out the line you wish to follow with a tacking stitch. Secure the end of the yarn at the right hand side. Insert the needle into the first

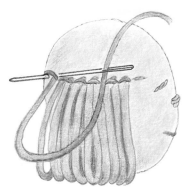

Long hair

Cut it across and secure strands together

Loops or fringe

stitch and pull the loop through to the length needed. Repeat this procedure until the fringe has been made, making sure each loop is even. Cut and trim a fringe but leave the loops as they are for a beard, mane, etc.

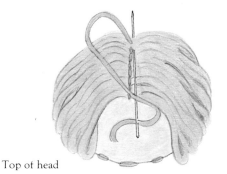

Top of head

Embroidery stitches
The main stitches used in this book are:
Lazy daisy – used for flowers.
French knots – used for the centre of flowers, eyes, noses, dots, warts, etc.
Satin stitch – used for eyes and noses.
Couch or feather (stem) stitch in a straight or curved line for a mouth.

For chain stitch work rows of lazy daisy

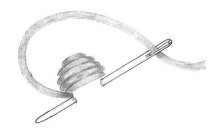

Satin stitch

French knot

Feather or stem stitch

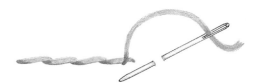

Couch stitch

Using embroidery for features
When not using felt for faces, etc, work the above embroidery stitches as follows: For eyes, work 4 lines of satin stitch over 1½ stitches; 4 lines for a nose over 2 stitches; 2 lines of satin stitch for eyebrows; a line of couch or feather stitching for a mouth, worked in a semi-circle.

OTHER IDEAS FOR EYES, MOUTHS AND NOSES

Eyes

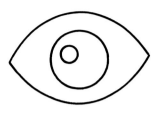

Noses and mouths for animals

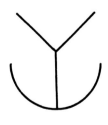

Mouths for dolls

Straight lines

Feather stitch

Satin stitch

Fabric with line sewn across

Features using felt
These can be either sewn or glued in place. For toys for very small children and babies make sure all features are sewn on very securely.

Working from diagrams
In each case, trace off from the actual diagram, cutting out the number stated. The seam allowance is ¼in (6mm) and has been included in the diagrams.

Sewing in felt
Felt is the best fabric to use as the edges require no finishing. To sew pieces together use a running or back stitch.

Acknowledgements
All yarns in this book were kindly
supplied by Patons Coats plc.
In the event of difficulty in obtaining
their yarn, please write to:
Patons Coats plc
PO Box 22
Darlington
Co. Durham
England DL1 1YQ.

All ribbons were kindly supplied by
Offray Ribbons plc.
In the event of difficulty in obtaining
their ribbons, please write to:
Offray Ribbons plc
Ashbury,
Rosecrea,
Co. Tipperary,
Ireland
Tel: Ireland 0505 21811

Patterns were checked by Peggy Greedus
and Margaret Furlong